Rome

Jessica Rudolph

Consultant: Karla Ruiz, MA
Teachers College, Columbia University
New York, New York

BEARPORT
PUBLISHING

New York, New York

Credits

Cover, © Prochasson Frederic/Shutterstock; TOC Top, © Lefteris Papaulakis/Shutterstock; TOC Bottom, © Vladimir Mucibabic/Shutterstock; 4–5, © S.Borisov/Shutterstock; 7, © Alena 11/Shutterstock; 8L, © Duncan Walker/iStock; 8–9, © Belenos/Shutterstock; 10, © Belenos/Shutterstock; 11T, © Maridav/Shutterstock; 11B, © Roger Bacon/REUTERS/Alamy Stock Photo; 12, © Stefano Carocci Ph/Shutterstock; 13T, © Michelangelo Oprandi/Dreamstime; 13B, © Walencienne/Shutterstock; 14T, © Travnikovstudio/Dreamstime; 14B, © GUIZIOU Franck/Hemis/Alamy Stock Photo; 15, © JM Travel Photography/Shutterstock; 16–17, © Neirfy/Shutterstock; 17R, © neneo/Shutterstock; 18, © RPBaiao/Shutterstock; 19, © vvoe/Shutterstock; 20L, © MNStudio/Shutterstock; 20–21, © Madzia71/iStock; 22 (Clockwise from TR), © ROMAOSLO/iStock, © Javen/Shutterstock, © Stefano Carocci Ph/Shutterstock, © vvoe/Shutterstock, and © Belenos/Shutterstock; 23 (T to B), © VDV/Shutterstock, © salajean/Shutterstock, © Duncan Walker/iStock, © Maridav/Shutterstock, and © Alliance/Shutterstock; 24, © Luciano Mortula/Shutterstock.

Publisher: Kenn Goin
Editor: J. Clark
Creative Director: Spencer Brinker
Photo Researcher: Thomas Persano

Library of Congress Cataloging-in-Publication Data

Names: Rudolph, Jessica, author.
Title: Rome / by Jessica Rudolph.
Description: New York, New York : Bearport Publishing, [2018] | Series: Citified! | Includes bibliographical references and index.
Identifiers: LCCN 2017010073 (print) | LCCN 2017010616 (ebook) | ISBN 9781684022359 (library) | ISBN 9781684022892 (ebook)
Subjects: LCSH: Rome (Italy)—Juvenile literature.
Classification: LCC DG804.2 .R84 2018 (print) | LCC DG804.2 (ebook) | DDC 945.6/32—dc23
LC record available at https://lccn.loc.gov/2017010073

For more information, write to Bearport Publishing Company, Inc., 45 West 21st Street, Suite 3B, New York, New York 10010. Printed in the United States of America.

10 9 8 7 6 5 4 3 2 1

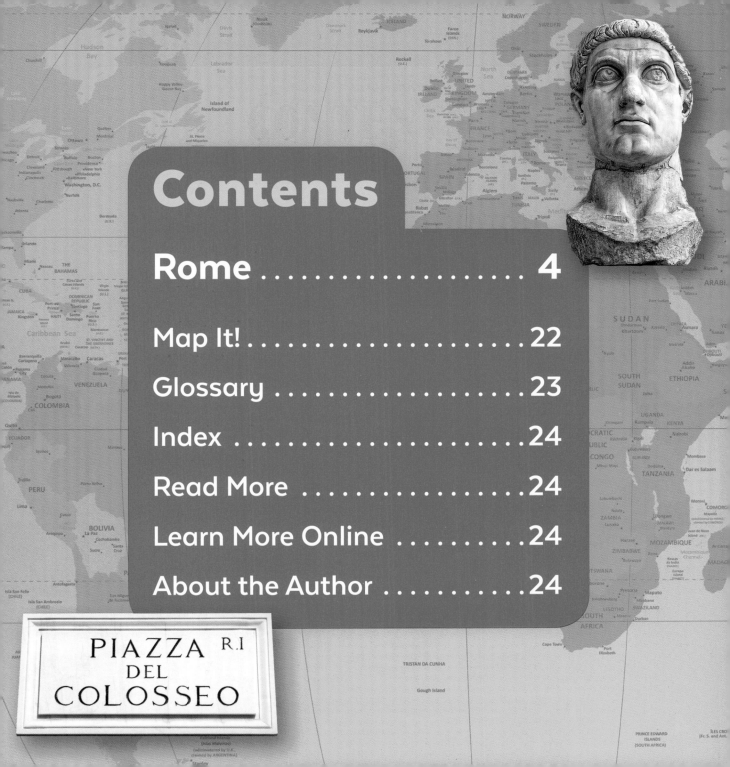

Contents

PIAZZA R.I
DEL
COLOSSEO

Welcome to

ROME

The Eternal City!

Eternal means "lasting forever."

Rome is the largest city in Italy.

More than two million people live there!

Rome is also the **capital** of Italy.

The Colosseum is a huge stadium in the city.

Long ago, big crowds watched **gladiators** fight to the death there!

The Colosseum was built about 2,000 years ago.

One of the most famous fountains in the world is Rome's Trevi Fountain.

Lots of **tourists** toss coins over their shoulders into the water.

They believe this **ritual** will guarantee that they'll one day return to Rome.

About $3,000 in coins are thrown into the fountain each day! The coins are collected every night and given to charity.

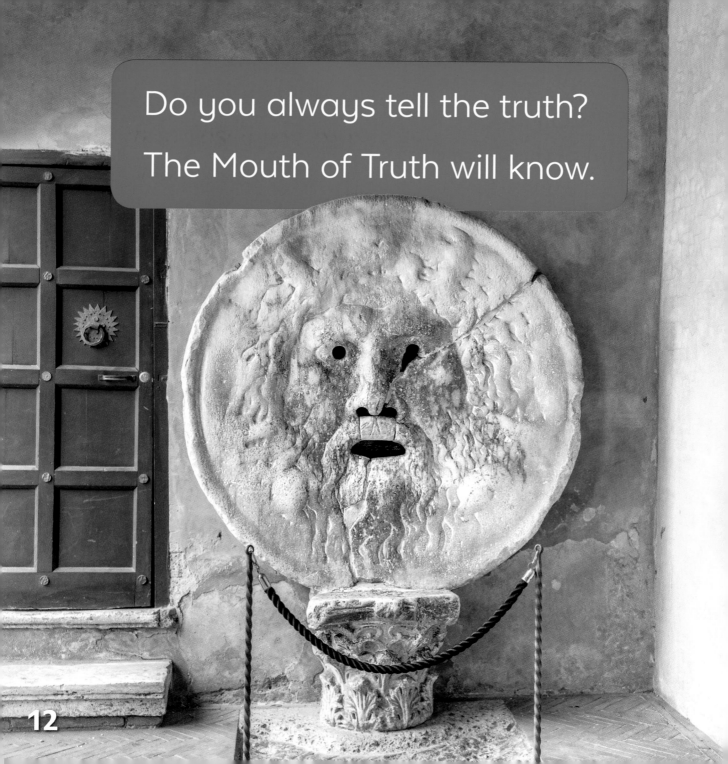

Do you always tell the truth?

The Mouth of Truth will know.

Stick your hand in the mouth of this large stone face.

Legend says that if you are a liar, your hand will be gobbled up!

The Mouth of Truth is located at the Church of Santa Maria in Cosmedin.

For a sweet snack in Rome, try gelato—Italian ice cream.

You can mix different flavors.

A shop where gelato is sold is called a *gelateria* (jeh–*lah*–teh–REE–ah).

Flavors of gelato include mango, vanilla with chocolate shavings, and super chocolate. *Yum!*

There's an entire country inside Rome called Vatican City.

It's only 109 acres (44 ha).

Fewer than 1,000 people live in Vatican City!

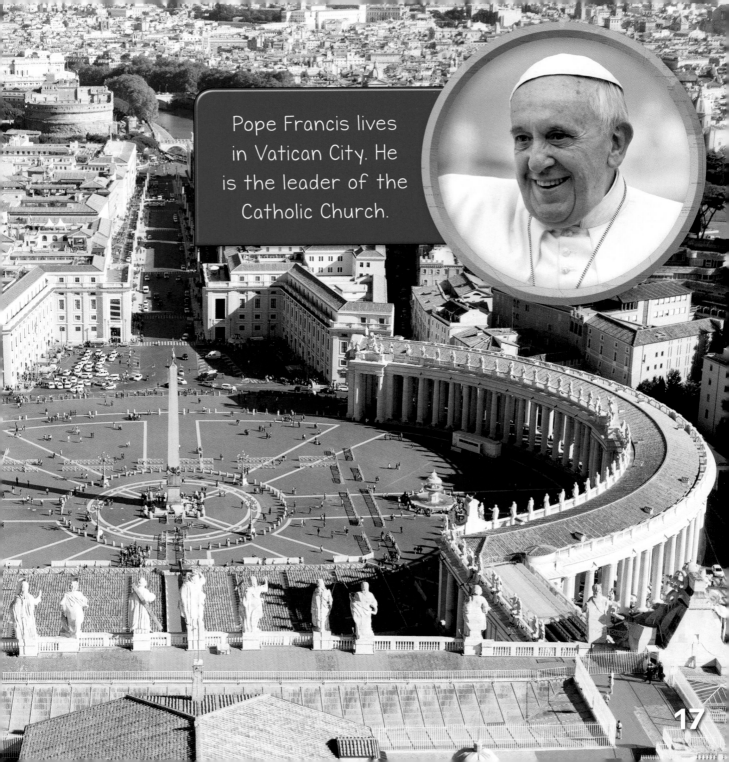

Pope Francis lives in Vatican City. He is the leader of the Catholic Church.

17

There are amazing works of art in Vatican City.

An artist named Michelangelo designed the dome on a church called St. Peter's Basilica.

Michelangelo lived from 1475 to 1564.

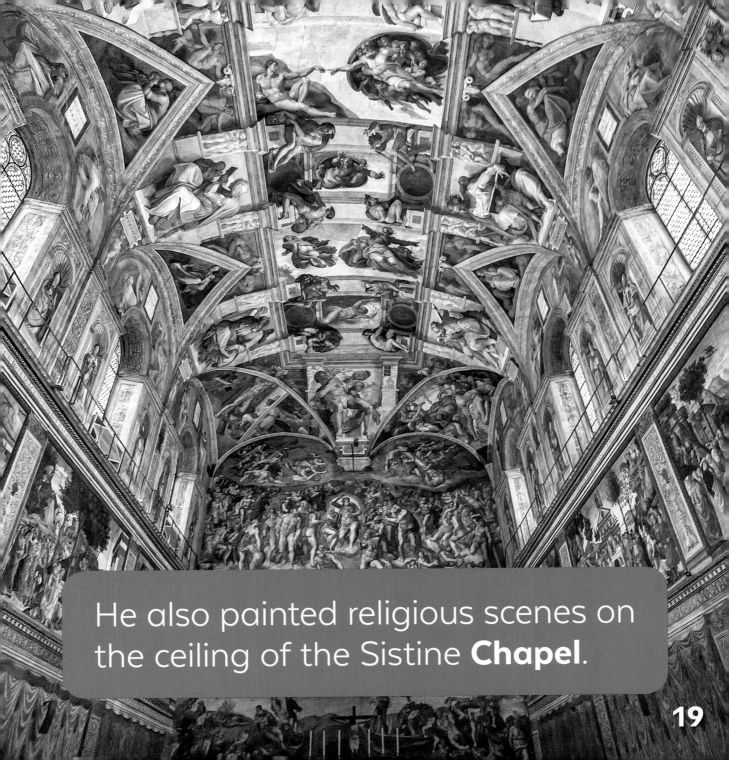

He also painted religious scenes on the ceiling of the Sistine **Chapel**.

After an exciting day of sightseeing, it's time to relax.

Head over to the Spanish Steps.

Huge crowds gather there.

Watch people go by or take a selfie!

The huge staircase has 135 steps.

MAP IT!
Rome

Trevi Fountain

Spanish Steps

Tiber River

St. Peter's Basilica

Mouth of Truth

Colosseum

Cool Fact:
When it was built, the Colosseum could hold about 80,000 people.

capital (KAP-uh-tuhl) a city where a country's government is located

chapel (CHAP-uhl) a building or room used for praying

gladiators (GLAD-ee-ay-turz) people who engaged in public fights to the death in ancient Rome

ritual (RICH-oo-uhl) a ceremonial act

tourists (TOOR-ists) people who travel to and visit places for pleasure

23

Index

Read More

Biesty, Stephen, and Andrew Solway. *Rome: In Spectacular Cross-Section.* Oxford: Oxford University Press (2004).

Lamprell, Klay. *Rome: Everything You Ever Wanted to Know (Not-For-Parents).* Oakland, CA: Lonely Planet (2011).

Learn More Online

To learn more about Rome, visit
www.bearportpublishing.com/Citified

About the Author

Jessica Rudolph lives in Connecticut. She has edited and written many books about history, science, and nature for children.